To Shreya,
Love and
happy reading!
Love,
Aunt Kath
2/03

This book belongs to:

• •

ISBN: 978-1-78324-265-8

Book design by Wordzworth
www.wordzworth.com

Paddy Platypus
This One's For You

Story by
Susan McCray

Illustrated by
David Calabrese

To Franceska, my mom, beautifully talented,
creatively inspiring, and who always made me feel special,

To Harry, my dad. who knew how to create and
play music that made people feel special,

To all children who have ever felt different,
know you are special,

To Cheryl, a kindhearted educator who
inspired me and the children she has known,

And to Kent, the love of my life who filled my days with love,
joy, generosity and understanding, a special man
loved by all who had the opportunity to know him.

Scan the QR code below and
use these lyrics to sing along...

https://www.paddyplatypus.com/

Perfect in pink Paddy Paddy
Purple and blue
Piano to play Paddy Paddy
Perfect are you

Pigtails and Bow Paddy Paddy
Perfect are you
Special are you, Paddy Paddy
This one's for you

Once upon a time there was a platypus named Paddy Platypus. Paddy was an only platypup living with her parents Paul and Petula Platypus in Pacoima.

Paddy would swim in the river nearby but wasn't happy because Paddy wasn't accepted by any of the other animals who swam and played there.

Many of the animals thought Paddy was different and rather peculiar, and didn't look at all like the other ducks, beavers or otters.

Paddy has a paddle shaped tail like the beaver, a sleek furry body like an otter, and a flat bill and webbed feet like a duck, but no other particular characteristics in common.

Paddy's particular pals were Peter Piper, the Penguin, and Petunia Pig. They liked and enjoyed being with Paddy unlike the Prickly Pamela Porcupine who made fun of Paddy and called her peculiar. Petunia Pig asked Paddy if she wanted to play with the other animals and Paddy told her she didn't want to do things with them because they made fun of her.

Paddy loved music and would dream about music, probably because her mother, Petula, would sing Paddy a lullaby before going to sleep. The song was pretty and the words very special.

Perfect in pink Paddy Paddy
Purple and blue
Piano to play Paddy Paddy
Perfect are you

Pigtails and Bow Paddy Paddy
Perfect are you
Special are you, Paddy Paddy
This one's for you

Every day Paddy would pretend to play the piano. Paddy hoped maybe one day to have a piano of her own on which she could possibly play a few favorite pieces by the composer Puccini, or a song sung by Elvis Presley, or a melody from the opera Pirates of Penzance, or even the lullaby Petula would sing called Paddy Paddy Perfect are you.

Paddy loved to go swimming. One day while perusing for a new spot in the water in which to paddle around Paddy spotted a piano and swam up to it. She put her webbed feet and wide bill on the piano and started to play.

Paddy gave the piano a name, Pizzicato! Pizzicato became as close as a best friend. Using Pizzicato, Paddy practiced and practiced until she could play her pieces perfectly. The piano made Paddy feel special, it was a blessing, and brought light to Paddy in its own unique way.

Paddy's particular pals, Petunia Pig and Peter Piper, told everyone how beautifully Paddy could play her piano, Pizzicato. Soon all gathered around to listen. It was only when she was praised as a pianist did others begin to respect her for her differences and how extremely special she really was. Paddy was a protégé, a platypus with potential, promise and possibilities to achieve great things.

Paddy's parents, Paul and Petula, were very proud. Petula made certain Paddy wore something in her favorite colors when she played her piano pieces for everyone. Paddy chose to wear a purple dress and pink pinafore with her hair in pigtails with a big pink bow.

To celebrate playing her piano, Paddy invited her playmates to gather together and partake in a picnic. They sat under the pergola in the park. Peter Piper, the Penguin, brought pickled peppers and pepperoni pizza without pineapple. Petunia Pig brought peanut butter on pumpernickel, and Paddy brought penne pasta with pesto and pancakes with peaches for dessert. It was a perfect party!

Paddy's pet parakeet named Penelope would go along practically everywhere with Paddy. Penelope enjoyed listening to Paddy play her music and would often sing along. Penelope's voice sounded as pretty as a piccolo. Of course, Paddy brought Penelope to the picnic and packed her favorite foods; pistachios and pretzel pieces.

People thought Paddy Platypus was peculiar and different, but playing Pizzicato taught Paddy that being different was a great thing for it meant she was special. It was when Paddy played the piano she found peace and tranquility and a happy place.

Paddy's personality exhibited a plethora of kindness, grace and bravery which found her a special place in the world. She brought beauty, laughter and music wherever she went. The music Paddy and Pizzicato created made others realize the gift that Paddy had as a pianist. They recognized the kindness she demonstrated by sharing her gift, as well as the pleasure it gave to others as they listened to her play her musical pieces. Paddy's performances proved that a "difference" is truly a special gift, unique to the individual, to be recognized and respected, but most importantly to be shared with others.

Paddy and her particular pals learned that each of them had a unique design, and the difference in the design of each creature should be celebrated and embraced. Even Pamela Porcupine, with her prickly personality, and who had always picked on Paddy, became personable.

Paddy Platypus was asked to perform at the Pavilion in Pacoima. Paddy decided it would be a perfect opportunity. In front of the Pavilion, and in the press, it proclaimed Paddy Platypus would be featured playing her piano, Pizzicato. Invitations went out to creatures near and far which read, "Presenting the piano artistry of Paddy Platypus with her best friend Pizzicato, playing Paddy's favorite pieces and a special encore performance of a lullaby her mother sang to her every evening, called Paddy Paddy".

18

The evening of the performance Paddy, wearing a purple pinstriped suit, welcomed everyone and introduced Pizzicato.
She played each piano piece flawlessly for the enjoyment of the crowd.

When it came to performing her encore piece, Paddy invited everyone to sing along with her and to sing the lullaby every day as a reminder that all creatures are perfectly special in their own way.

CPSIA information can be obtained
at www.ICGtesting.com
Printed in the USA
LVHW071450170223
739769LV00011B/418